PRAISE FOR *IS IS ENOUGH*

Lauren Camp has the perfect touch. Her precise, exquisitely tuned poems lean us into scenes and understandings that feel both riveting and enduring . . . her poems deepen the world.
—NAOMI SHIHAB NYE

Lauren Camp's new book is a stubborn testimonial to existence, to the sufficiency of life as it is in all its messy dailiness. I am moved by the speaker's central struggle, which is her desperate attempt to hold onto and let go of her beloved father who held on even as he lost his memory, his history, himself. *Is Is Enough* is a tenacious elegy-in-the-making, a book of being standing against nothingness.
—EDWARD HIRSCH

PRAISE FOR *LAUREN CAMP*

Camp distills grief, loss, and transition, each becoming a kind of theft, and the poems strive to reclaim and recover what can be salvaged.
—*Publishers Weekly*

Scope, complexity, and amplitude—a work of fine poetic intelligence.
—*Rain Taxi Review of Books*

It's as if Camp has reached into the collective unconscious and pulled out ribbons of spirit memory that, at some point, each of our souls knew.
—*World Literature Today*

Every time I read Lauren Camp, I'm reminded of how extraordinary she is—the complexities managed with sophistication and grace.
—*Washington Independent Review of Books*

The poems knew something about me, something I didn't know, or couldn't articulate. The poems did the saying, the impossible saying, for me.

—*The Rumpus*

One of the most sensuous books you'll ever read and characteristic of the gorgeousness of [Camp's] work.

—*Electric Lit*

Lauren Camp's poetry is remarkable for its ability to bend time, its unexpected word choices and collage of extreme landscapes, ordinary events and bold feeling statements.

—*Tupelo Quarterly*

Each poem gives us a breath of obsession, a moment to relish in the moment, a detail, a piece, a way to know something in a world where knowledge is ever fleeting.

—*Cultural Daily*

Camp holds space for us all to be observers, adventurers, poets even, while showing us the benefits of paying attention to the world around us and embracing the vastness of darkness.

—*Psaltery & Lyre*

A stunning collection . . . [the poems'] music and imagery makes them at once easily accessible and endlessly minable.

—*Poetry Matters*

Camp's work is endlessly soulful, its lines slipping between emotions, memories and scenes to show how each is made up of the other.

—*Columbia Daily Tribune*

Lauren Camp is not only a talented poet of national renown, but a gifted teacher with exciting ideas about how to engage the people of New Mexico in the writing, reading, and overall enjoyment of poetry.

—MICHELLE LAFLAMME-CHILDS, Executive Director, New Mexico Arts

IS IS ENOUGH

IS IS ENOUGH
POEMS

LAUREN CAMP

21st Century Poets, No. 43

★trp TRP: The University Press of SHSU
Huntsville, Texas 77341

Library of Congress Cataloging-in-Publication Data

Name: Camp, Lauren author
Title: Is is enough : poems / Lauren Camp.
Other titles: 21st century poets no. 43.
Description: First edition. | Huntsville, Texas : TRP: The University Press
    of SHSU, 2026. | Series: 21st century poets ; no. 43
Identifiers: LCCN 2025034710 (print) | LCCN 2025034711 (ebook) | ISBN
    9781680034523 trade paperback | ISBN 9781680034530 ebook
Subjects: LCSH: Senile dementia--Poetry | LCGFT: Poetry
Classification: LCC PS3603.A4559 I85 2026 (print) | LCC PS3603.A4559
    (ebook)
LC record available at https://lccn.loc.gov/2025034710
LC ebook record available at https://lccn.loc.gov/2025034711

FIRST EDITION

Cover art: Uta Barth, *Ground 30*, 1994, Ektacolor print on panel, 22 x 18 inches; 55.8 x 45.7 cm, Edition 4 of 8, 2
APs. Courtesy the artist and Tanya Bonakdar Gallery, New York / Los Angeles.
Author photo by Bob Godwin

Cover design by Alban Fischer
Interior design by Maureen Forys, Happenstance Type-O-Rama

Printed and bound in the United States of America
First Edition Copyright: 2026

TRP: The University Press of SHSU
Huntsville, Texas 77341
texasreviewpress.org

Let us be gentle when we question our fathers.
ANNE CARSON

CONTENTS

ص

ON HARMONY

Train stops and eggplant and the grim little sun and our clapping
all morning and later we slicked down to righteous
dance moves, pink greasy boxes of dough. Some would say

we were not divine between us but we hummed our shared holy
family in a quarry of folding chairs. One hour skimmed
to another and they were not forbidden, or clarified

with reason, but the ache of the olives and responses
rendered in timbal, qanun, tarub, the oud, and the sounds again
of distress and truth. Darwish said "Nothing is harder . . . than the smell

of dreams while they're evaporating." On those days we dressed
in our blacks and thick tongues, and the narrative
we offered was not an acceptance, a raging. We wanted to forget

to kneel. We spent the days linked to our divisions
of oppression and we fixed to the matter
of beginning. Every thought claimed five wounds. Dresses loose

with their fine threads, red and lime,
wheat gold. Outside, a stone bridge watched the great river
weeping; a mother sang to her baby. My taste in the mouth

of this crowd. *Habibi*, our losses, and most of us rustling
our arrows beneath them. Five times a day we ate the oily
sweetness with our vigorous fingers, our tongues moving to cumin

and cream, and we passed from news to a chapel
of pita, to portions of dusk, our ghosts and marginal angers.
I took 48 photos of shadows in quick succession,

thinking one better than another, and saw in each photo
a lapse to spot evidence. I deleted them
from my memory which wanted not to hunger

for these compulsions, statistics. We were taught
so many instances to doubt, but the light came along
singing and we joined it, taking its melody as apology.

ص

SANCTUARY

I collect another phrase
for safekeeping. No need to do more
than hold his fragrance: egg, anger, each thick
river of rejoicing. On my fridge, a scrap
of my father, his perfect print
which held all the black of a day
and its losses. Now he learns the equation
for why I tell him this beginning.
From the first morning of my childhood
when he lifted me up, with iron
in his body and my apple-sized eyes. My father,
I looked giddy and exhaled.
That was Sunday. The village. I was a baby sugared
with indulgence. Fat and black-haired. Those years
of his unfolding wallet and the ongoing thorn
of origin. We knocked on the heavens
with our knees. Such boredom.
These days, the body holds its heat.
We begin with my name: a portrait of belonging.
We pantomime conversation.
I never want to feel more than I do. No,
it isn't that. Twitching all night again. Is his presence more
of a parting or a start? My father.
I separate each hollow. I always knew
four months of snow. We bought sweaters,
he tested my algebraic solutions, my mother danced
in our hotel rooms. Her arms were pale.
If train A and train B are traveling at different speeds
from two different cities
what is the time before collision? My father.
I am not looking for a way out.

PLOT SUMMARY

Had I known anything teachers wouldn't have taught me
    civil wars branches of government Iroquois longhouses teachers
most days said how to scrape from their mouth what was
    ancient trident or surrendered habitat and would know
that the spill of formaldehyde gave us webbed frogs
    to dissect geologic shrines how to tune a flute so much
negative capability in me I couldn't play notes even as instructed yet
    without learning I memorized seasonal notches like drowning
rain with its gathering monologues of noise on my attic or summer's
    waxed petals a jeweled delusion that took the whole side
of the house by the basketball hoop safe to say all
    my childhood I came in the back door spinning
silly fragments of babble and sticks and exhibits of growing
    and never thought more than the center
of my bed in the attic watching crackup sitcoms
    when our dog died I was in Israel and my parents
didn't object when I thinned to a plane but when I
    drifted into the ribs of the west in my green outfits and brushes
they reminded me the pot was always cooking
    basmati and meat in the broiler flattening frying
left me queasy I molted from them and talked
    only of moonlight and David's topaz eyes so my mother flew
over to see who this was and investigated his proceedings
    a divorce sketched as near completion but wait
for a year my father grew a beard I was three and scared
    of his face which I couldn't see
from some threshold he had returned from
    land in the middle east he brought me lions the gravel to start
a conversation my grandma gave me gold
    bracelets that dragged on my little wrist and later some parakeets
clustered in our dining room a room
    we only used to cut my brother's penis on a silver

tray and over years appendages broke
	and were fixed in Oklahoma we had stitches staples and still
police came to the door twice three times to see that
	my parents stopped whatever harm I was born
under an arch because my father needed to close
	his black book the rush to two women each
weekday needed the domestic we never parked at the subway I got
	older with his ancient coins had to practice
my daring in private let my hands feather
	body while the tin sky
yawned I hardly remember what it was like to be young but I
	know when my mother was fertile she fell into
the cellar after that she stayed a large
	shadow on the bed many months overlooking
the newspaper she must have been waiting
	for vague woes on our dim cul-de-sac this bell
of memory rings through me.

From what has started in autumn bristles, very numerous, not listed here.
Let's throughout and until half. Or let's go backward.

I PULL INTO THE WALGREENS PARKING LOT

To elapse this story means to knifework & life-ease
the unbearable. So when he calls, instead of driving, I sit hushed
in this repeated city beside the embarrassed trees, too much

concrete pigment. My father outlines his now-failure
& death & discontinue. Again, again, whatever won't quit
his mind: the bike the bag the way the seat

made people disappear. All the while, the body
of with & against buds without nouns, but I know
his crammed overgrown frets that hasten

to anger. The dashboard clock goes on, the same numbers
re-ordered. He tells me how he fingerknicks his scalp
of its allegiant spots & I love that head

that's sun-indulgent, that orphans its smallest terrors. I watch
people walk along the nearby folds of road. An hour
through his joists of memory. My fingers fish my purse

for random dirty sweets. I'm seeing through glass
how we were five & sweaters & faith
wide enough to sing God's names & later down

to one, one, one, one. I have to figure
he is an old man hammering dozens of times
on the story & its contamination. The whole city can see me

sitting here as his words curve to my throat. I take them,
take them; you can't want a man to be quiet without
stuttering with death. The words back-to-back flint

every next thought. You might think I wait for every clump
of foul from his pockets. I can't stop the time
to headlong my silence. There are days breaking this blood. Days after

to slip under its flank. That's why I'm in a parking lot
holding my hand in my tired hand & saying
love, the word stuck to my palm. This teaches me

not to hurry & this is not enough. *Love, love*
& again the traffic light burns up with red. The sky falls
toward night. Saying it in every available absence.

ELEGY FOR THE ROUTINE

The future wants to stay alone—
a small box with small items,
but we are broke down
to his daylight swervings,
the extension of two dimensions
and the narrows from his mouth to door.
Fricatives flick through my headset.
Unless you know he is flying
into the last part in danger
of attack from inside, unless you know
our work of slaying apparitions,
you might ask the event:
body, love, unceasing taxes,
the freeway? Every thought bright
and lost. To understand willing
we must not know our anxiety. It is punishment
to hear the swift pitch of some pauses.
I was about to go, he said
and *Don't,* I reply, respectful
of the code of his upkeep.
In the mornings my sister writes
with her fidgety worries. Again
the breath of the ruined clock
and we wander
the tall sound of trust as it loosens.
Is he eating?
Soon evening and swallows,
and after most of the last laments,
we let him carry on
with his inclinations while the glass trees
keep rising,
one day and one day
toward the least. His voice unzips

the few words he has formed
for this purpose, what he says
of coming apart. All together a dictionary
of five seasons, eight years
or some other steady rate
of invisible sticking
points. After loneliness, there remains
great loneliness. We speak its narrative
every morning. *I've had a good day*
and I don't know how to solve it.
If we must exterminate
our house-sized blame,
let the heart move
to the hereafter. Tell me to be
at the mall listening
to his slap splitting
the phone line. Every fragment of this
story is true. Every day all its strange
exhalations. A conversation
that bends. Sometimes I can't
identify all the right
angles, but in my notebook
I write his daily fixations. My brother says
it sounds like his brain is breaking
and the forgetting of pleasure
takes my ear. But more than that. Every line
that lets us be family. The images turn
and I hold them. I want
to repair them. If we both could
see him, he'd be sitting
in a tired suit
rattling his fingers while a shofar blasts
the underside of awe,

of rising and letting go. The suit on the chair
as the sun nearly depleted weeps
into violet. The suit and the touch
of intrusion. We hurry off
to make words in another
room. Several people keep peering
in our windows, and we're missing
composure. The unsaid hope
all broken. Again with
the experimental drug and how many bottles
we've committed to. The tablets
—white, oblong—
the mind of the suit to be worn.
Motionless, we try to stop the edges
from lurking, the crack of suspicion that keeps
aiming its brass at rows and strokes
from long ago and his inadequate
aim. All truth is the signature
static on paper, the worn suit
of the mind. What he says
is to anyone now
with its shaky brightness. The mind
is geography. The mind is the giant
and its incessant informing
is final. I return
to the messages and how he wept. Desire to
tenderness. The past is bending over
to see what is no longer
there. When he is this far
out of focus, we pay for his money money
and more money. *Are they poisoning—?*
No, now I see the corner,
muttering. Around him, x-ed selves

who keep tossing him stones.
This means you will think it hurts
to love. But no. This is the tall sound
of summer getting paler. How do I know
that this man with redundance will still
breathe at the shore
of his thoughts? I want
correct answers. Then calm. And the afternoons
leak to a house of ranunculi
or ubiquitous Florida. Enough later
to care. He wouldn't go
and then wouldn't not. The flap
of his staggers and glitters
of memory. Stubborn. My sister and I take up
the rumple of praying
without supervision.
A woman has the will
and sends his will—without a wrinkle
through the mail. We make it through
the weekend with all its singing,
then receive every email
with *again*. More very old
grimaces. Notes (mine)
and loops (his). *Have you heard—?*
The shoved-in ellipses. Time repeats
its September, October,
and meanwhile only hours. Then September
a lot. The fear
that we are reducing
life to a suit jacket.
It's all he has. Into the *again*
again. Every necessary name, the opposite,
oppositive. The names he knew

dangling. The straightened names
unmanned. We tell him
in thin moments, and he slips
beyond them. After hours and days his freedom
is sweaty. He is criticized for the shock
of his odor. Prepared to show better
he sits soaped in the shower
after a tantrum. Time in and out,
soaking and heavy. Now
he's by the ocean and is marveling
at his old habits. Or he's advancing the car
over cobblestones
to a corner. He can no longer
drive. Between terraces, he unfurls
a hat and walks window
after window. The immense city. He dresses
in beige day after day. Tells the sister, the cousin
what he can't remember:
every fault as it escalates. He's off
to the temple wearing his
threadbare jacket. The rest of the year begins
today. It moves around
and we attempt to restore it. My sister
texts more inaudible news. I can't
concentrate. The emails end
in hours and there's nothing in front
for me to cross back from.
He calls. It's night now. Somewhere
he hangs up. We keep talking, the words
subdividing. I sleep with his face
in the case of my brain. Sparrow
and anger from a blanket through night, flailing
limbs. Nowhere more blackness. He knows

my name is something that was said
earlier. The next day is launched
loud from a distance. I swear
to sift through the depths
when the holiday is over. I promised
we could be in the city
of love without reason and this most of all
will not save him. He tells me who
he is. Good dad.
This is every tree. This is gravel; look
at the sunset. Look how the blues spread
through his suit jacket. Blues
browse our names. Time is entirely shallow
sounds. Those last daylight hours
eat and eat and morning comes,
rearranged. What's been praised are the margins
of childhood, the pulp
of our old tudor, two years
and all the clocks
disillusioned of new possibility,
the drain and the bugs that came up,
winging. His mind ate the language. Language eats
every landmark, and now
we're all smudges. Can't more blur
house or ransack what's stuck
in its nest. Love is each
complicated sadness. A checkbook
with holes in the sides. This will be the last move
to return. The prayers speaking
and he'll remember only the splinter
of nights and how rescue
became subtractions, and now
our abrupt coordination when he needs

absence. We practice mouth-blame
till he loosens. His mind refusing
to solve every fragment.
A weak cloud moves past
with the insignia of leaving.
We estimate, then go to twenty four-
seven, all the clocks back
to humming. A room. Many counters.
We used to say we didn't gamble.
Now we have to.
He shrugs. Does it have to be
constant? He utters another
tragedy. Each phone call is all sky, and then error
from the flesh of my heart. I am
what he cast, and my promise
is crooked. No *must* but all leaping. The cool
of the pane and later a scotch to calm
the hippocampus. Let it be
spacious where he stores his awkward
artifacts. Don't worry, we say
to ourselves. We'll get past
the ripeness. Every tree in this town
has been broadcasting
pollen. Even driving slow, we break
toward time with no
signs. Snow is already scratching
the ground. Check the seasons
and let out their flutters.

SMEARY FLOWERS, 1983

All I wanted was the haze of a worn gown
              of sleep after the scrape of that
       honey-sipped night. I lay back
on the seat to the space around thinking, to the stitch
              of each parcel and limb. That night

of my uncle's second wedding, I was
              afforded small space in the bark
       of the city's indifference, given
the middle of the road as the ambulance threw
              black rings of sound toward

the ear of the borough. Something needed
              breaking. My soft wrist
       on the reed of my arm. From this distance
of decades, I know that was the side
              of my life I was wearing. The wavering

silk. The tender demeanor. Canting night
              nuzzling tendons and bones
       as Dad drove, and the wheels strewed
in the drizzle. I had lapsed into dozing
              the rippled bowls

and gold coins of the belly dancers'
              wide centers unwrapping eddies
       of notes—circular, pulsing,
a physical singing. When the frame of our car
       stapled its metal to the side

of another, the road
                painted sky with lights on the back
        passenger window, a shower of smeary
red flowers. Blood glistened
        like buttons from a gash

on the downhill side of my father's
                steep forehead. Someone moaned,
        someone in shadow—my mother perhaps,
adding to the dissonant drone
        of the city, the violet danger,

its crisscross of midnight. And winter
                kept speaking. That night
        was never bent on farewell. It continued;
the doctor washed his hands
        before stepping back to the traumatized

hall, to the reign of one hospital's fluorescence.
                That's all there was—
        After my uncle's second wedding,
my family's brown Buick spun
        slowly toward home. I was slumped

in the back, my brother beside me
                in the hem between seats. Us,
        in our childhood, the division
of heartbeats, and the ever slippery
        dark, cascading through windows.

GOODBYE TO AGGRESSIONS AND GENEROUS GESTURES

Every visit he didn't and didn't and then could
able less. This was an extravagant
minimum we'd come to expect. Winter is endless

tight branches. I remember his voice as a nation, all the doors
shutting and us eating
our behaviors. Sorry citizens. Evenings, the street
                                        loosed out my small windows.
                          Name something that seems perfect.

I'm telling you my father's silence, every mobbing of it. Not telling
the clamor for days of unused parts
of our hope. Kafka wrote, *A cage went in search of a bird.*

I don't know if I'm lonely.
                          Name the doorway, then walk through.

Not to tongue more than he can, I hurry to listen. With vanishing,
he has removed each pronoun of home. He still wants
                    to name
                    swerve and siege, pause and anthem.

I sit beside him in the thrift and watch it froth.
Love is a habit. Then a moon. A spatter
of color priming the treetops. I laugh about the moon. He laughs.

When he laughs, there is so much
of him—multiple pieces: and, of, or, if. What are our names?

                    The lock, the solution. Name it all.

RECLAIMING PERSPECTIVE

Confession: the week after you saw him, he walked
through the city's headlights
in a suit. A stranger

returned him through pinpricks of sunrise. And again.
And again—with calls each time
to report his aimless shadow.

He could end anywhere and it's that absolute
that scared me. You want to believe I'm shame-
sewn, faulty. You want to know

why he's in there? Do you think I don't see
the other residents nod off or pace out
broken thoughts? I'm grateful now

the doors fight back. He must not amble to the pitch
of a whim. Oh he's durable, my father,
but each day he wakes with a little less

truth. Or truth that won't help him.
His window looks to a lodged plum tree.
He no longer repeats

his regrets. His small room
is grand enough to put his name on the wall
six times. He has enough space

in his day and mind for unpredictable syllables
and stock prices that roll and saddle
his screen. They gleam, painless.

Misnomers and "accidents" no longer
torment him. True, he has bones
for concrete. Sometimes his old city creeps over his face.

I can't break him of that. I had to decide
how far to unravel. For months, he piled unopened mail
on his bed, size-sorted. All September he gorged

on weeping. I wanted to wake knowing
that the dark hadn't held him
at knifepoint. Believe me—his life is a lot

to absorb. I still expect him to remember to sleep
and kiss and mete or shutter the sun
when it chunks through his windows. Let soon

not come yet to his doorway. In phone calls, he pulls out
any name that sounds about right. We laugh
at his small creases, and the losses

don't scare me like they did. Maybe I'm paying
for him to be outlined in the blousy sun
and to cup casual melodies each night.

Nothing is insignificant, but I know the room
holds all his history. There's no doubt he's dipping below
membranes. I gather his failure

at the corners of my mouth
to use on relatives who intercede: *He's softening
to broad, precious pauses. He's safe,* I'll tell them.

Take the week he started wearing his socks
eight days in endless conservation, his toes grown
with fungus. Take the days he spoke

the immediate future as an ancient alphabet.
A time will come. His brain is dismantling,
but he isn't waiting. His identity is not where he left it.

I never want him to know
he's been wrong. He breathes through his teeth,
then takes them out. There's always crud

on the underside, and I'm so tired
and unprepared for this. How many rules and lessons
make a whole life? He can't say, but of course, I know.

HIS KINGDOM OF BROODING

Dad paced the 12x15 room with a green cap in his hand.
Only when he was bereft did he call.
His calls came unending.
Then, many messages.
We had bought him the recipe for safety.
He mumbled about the locks.
Now he could no longer travel the aisles of cloves.
Of course we apologized.
Each time we entered his room, he pulled open a drawer.
After that, another.
He named objects and light.
Each hour he saw different afternoons in panes of wide rectangles.
He called me *dear*, which was a shimmer.
The eggs came all runny, with biscuits.
And he made it clear he'd never take part in the singing
though he'd voice the familiar rhythm of anger.
He said he missed bread with crusts.
He did nothing each day, but the outside was pleasing.
Bougainvillea and mandolins, or that's how it seemed.
He was cleaned of all but the worries.
He had cigars but wanted only the tin.
He smoked in the garden and said they were worthless.
In his room he again walked in circles.
Could we return him the city? Concrete would do well, he reminded.
Could we drive him to places with outlines?
We were delicate in our answers.
We interrupted him, and his thoughts mingled, departed.
Dad used words like *otherwise* and *washed up*.
He wanted to organize paper clips in his old apartment.
We taped his beautiful face on the door
and told him to always turn left at the orchid.

EPISODIC PARALLELS, MORE AUNT, LESS MOON

Trucks muscle aggressions down Second, and I
race across, a little late, raising my arms in greeting. She sees
my form. How holy the eager heart. We move inside
the lean light of the diner. Her wide voice whittles
its tempers from thick pulp to diaphanous
weave. Had it not been for that, I mightn't have thought
to a far time when I was still milk and silly. When the moon
and its waxy white busted her open. The surge
of the Unification Church hung over—forcing, and she
followed its crescents. You know, back then there were two
verbs: trust and flight. *How much enough is enough,* my father asked
as he and my mother tugged her from plentiful failure,
from faith, unstitching her logic. Took her to the small
room she rented with a rectangle of couch
and bed, a plastic bin of albums: The Who, The Dead. Shifty
rug, a vase of wandering daisies. Again, she went
by the pigeons. Again, she stood with her soliloquies
and theories and candles at the airport, dealing
flowers. A focus, an axis. This was years ago. I couldn't
feel the orbit of shamans. Didn't know life had many
menus. I watched out the window at the journey. Now, here,
midday, midtown in this mustardy light, our hands loose
on Formica, she mentions memory as a suitcase and folds
into it only what she can carry. *Honey, do you want more,*
the waitress asks, a stained coffeepot in her hand. My aunt
shakes her full face. Hours turn willingly. All the past is the rest
of the garish city. At one point, we look to the streets
eager to overwhelm our eyes. To move off
the bruise of the worse lying still in our laps. What is life
but another loneliness, lights out? Our talk rises
and falls, becomes soft. Then we are done; we walk out
to everyone else's scene, look at the comma of street, look
to the low moon.

FORTUNE

I keep lists of plants and lists of the best of everything
else: lipsticks and Latvian streets and thrift stores
at every distance. I continue to think
it would be good to do some reliable fleeing.
I get ahead of myself,
seeking goodness at each next corner.
In September, I saw some of the space
on the surface of a desert:
a doll's house of sedums,
an abacus of seedlings. I smelled the familiar
artemisia, the vertigo of the bleeding
heart. We've lived in the same house
for a score but took out peas and foxgloves, put in
small greening truth, particulate amidst rust.
We've built many gardens and yesterday
crouched down to see what the plants have done
since the last time we crouched or dropped water on them.
And then we went to Tim's
and he made curry and we hovered over old memories
sucking the nectar out of them, trying to remember
if they were true or right.
Full, we sat on the couch that came with his tiny
place, and Tim showed us a ballet he had queued on his screen;
forty dancers skinned to transparencies,
bellying from hushed sounds to bending.
Tim had been away fourteen years.
Lived in Milwaukee near his mother.
He still has a globe of white hair.
Moment passes moment to make a lifetime.
I can no longer list the many people
I've been, all the proportion and practice:
breath and riddle worn soft.
It's a new day. We might get rain.

I dress in a shirt the color of sky
and other pale traces. I'll go outside.
The earth is full of surprises.
Dad once planted marigolds.

OUR DAILY RATION

The moon is brighter since the barn burned.
—Matsuo Bashō

Dad drifts through his clouds of surrounding
concerns. *I'm doomed*, he says to his phone. I laugh to remind him

the percussion of astonishment. To him I know everything

is abundant repetition. Photos of family, shells,
bread, an old hat and stopped watch
lawn his dresser. His drawers are furred

with paper towels folded in thirds between each black globe
of rolled sock. Too much

and less. A man storing escape.

I slice celery for the crock pot. Sigh in near perfect pitch
and my articulations verge on defiance.

I am now only chopping up silence, moving the small
pieces into a bowl. There is no wind
against my mouth. On the phone my father murmurs, *What do I need*

with this life? It is impossible to better
the words he rehearses. Can he hear me pretend?

I section each carrot on the diagonal. Peel the crisp white coat
from the garlic. Onion. Its transparent wings,
purple tears. I no longer cry, despite minimal inseparable hiding places.

I wipe down the cutting board.
Residue. Heat a spill of broth. My hands shape another
nourishment as if reason is eased by the slightest touch.

Nothing I can stop. The moon climbs the junipers
to look at me. White and alone. I calculate where Dad is

in this disease by what he blames. So many chances to tilt. Windows,
appetite. I bone fat away, drop in the cubed meat. Each day returns

with the thin exact blade
of my father's voice. What has been cut
from what he had yesterday. I stir the soup with a pine spoon. A breeze rivers
this desert from the east.
Because I know my father I know my father

is smiling and this is wrong. He puts the smile
to his mouth. Mountain sky. Adobe
holds its ordinary heat. I scratch scum from the still surface of the pot.

I taste the stock and realize the assumption
of apology. He pinches the closest word

and drops it into the phone. I swallow. *Hello*, I say again.

I am your oldest. I let that simmer. I don't understand
what his ear needs. What the mouth gives.
Leave it be, he repeats when he can't remember the source

of his thought. The sky is ceremonial.
His lips hold his own forgiveness. I stand at the stove in reveries. Frontal tangle,

nerve. Not grief
but autumn. Not grief but what speech has caused me

to defend. The hesitation stretches
its chant. The hesitation reaches
with an upper and lower. Everything I hear now overlaps. Points of time

the size of faint recollections, and these variations evolve
tender, quiet. Tomorrow he may sound

better. I introduce a final seasoning. Strew the meat
to ribbons. Soup at last. Soup always better the next day.

Here is a spoon. I made this.
Let's sit on these sides of the table.

Long ago I had a father; the familiar
was beginning. Later much later a prayer, a bowl.

THE DEVOTIONS

Sneezing and shiner-eyed in an entire landscape ripped
    by wind and today I wrestle
every negative planked in my inbox while finches feast on suet, rubbing
    round heads to each other, to glued
seed. March is and did and has just rained and now relentless
    tumbling hail. The desert is giddy
with moisture but still claims worst drought. News again
    spilled to oil and buzzing. Time grenades
these days a constant, so I hover
    over bean dishes, then drive my white car
under hawk-knifing and cloud-shrift. Let me not see
    the latest media fog on Facebook. How we fall to ruin
and futility. At the college today,
    after talking to that last student who wanted to burn
all his papers, to be someone better, I stopped to see the santos
    under glass in the hallway, narrow faces whittled
from cedar, clustered figures clasping their crosses,
    mythical. I circled the room, submitting
to exhaustion. I once didn't know the world
    holds harm. Now days line up and I hear
racketing fury. Around me, sun moves in
    and I am glad to have someone beloved
and imperfect. My mouth his mouth and no measure
    other than heart rate
can wound me. We live among acres with their evidence
    of tangling. On the way home, I pass pilgrims
earnest in their toil. The horizon holding good
    in front of me. It's easy to see
the ground fold in and turn purple. Some will find their way
    through lacerations. This is only one
truth I'll never know, and the small fates
    of who's plagued and whose life is saved.

STRANGERS IN OUR OWN EARTH

We have been made into something other:
something ancient, swallowed—

badland curves set from the once of subtropics,
maybe single-celled algae and zooplankton. Behind each cretaceous sea

we are the same buried peat. The desperate hunger
of crocodiles and turtles, those nubbed skins

affixed in suspension. What marks us is
the trapping of buried shale and siltstone, the early sternum

of existence. We are confessed
in installments, each realm rendered to gully

and splinter. Let me tell you, an eon
is one of my names. Name me in floating and flint,

mercy and sand. Name me bird,
detail, the very least. Name me the punishment

of history, what broke, what isn't still lit. Name me the water as it lifted up
what it could to make exiled artifact.

We have traveled a long way to dwell on colors
that lip our past. Fragments of struggle. Though it all seems faded

to inner layers, and no one
remembers what's nested, the story of dying is much more

than some parts swift vaulted. Time is not simple, not
quick pickled deterioration. I was an artist once.

Within me, perfect vibrance, twin constellations.
You could say the years constricted and then sank into silence. I stopped

and was lost for a storm then droned
a winter by the window. Every angry breath became

the same consistency. But to reshape, you hold what
hollers out from under you.

Some wings are left in the depth
and hogback ridges. Old reds prove safe-kept by compressing.

ص

PROGNOSIS

My father is all
at once. It is noon and widens
further into another
landscape of feet.
The words he uses are a measure
of the half-point
to silence. We listen
to the mirror on the wall
and my father is bent
down with
grizzle and returning
spaces. My father reminds me
of my father. Father
as conveyance, as legal
document, as night flight, lost
pitch. Next question. For something
to do, we name the body
by streaming daylight:
knee, nerve, stomach. Reason
the tender sound of sun. Name hope
as a pleasantry. We are spending
our time folded
into it, finding
ourselves. We are not
doing nothing. We are planning
the task of letting go
of all thought and my father is root
and tree. I put my hand
on his hand
and build a small
mountain. I haven't described
his voice. An hour passes again.
A sound not said. A negative

ghost. A rain
unbuckles the leaves.
Perhaps we'll look
in the mirror and see
what just happened—
what I mean
is, the future.

PROBABILITY: THREE CITIES, FOUR MINDS, DOUBLE ENTRY

They close the door lock the door so only we enter
Leave

Is there more—? The beck
of wind

I came through from snow and looked out the window
I walked past the fish to the orchid and entered his room
where he fitted where he folded

his slow set of plans

I opened his dresser admired his shirts with their broken collars
I admired the walls and he looked at the walls
I walked past the walls and tasted the soup

He forked through the soup and fastened

his eyes on the contradictions
Here are the weak thick pieces of thought we keep taking back

each hour stooped soft to another
and time still insists on a few sentences Suddenly we are talking

about a baby—how old?— the baby is most days
slow conversation The baby
is beautiful there is so much story and the baby

is continuous We push and pull
and rustle the horizon the
now and then

We laugh and this is enough furniture

What is inside as if making sense as if sorting

the day from the long up ahead
We name what we miss
Now this is our delicate father

GIVEN

Endlessly governed by the endless.
Tangled lines, private pause. Invaluable hours. This is all

worth repeating: the rise and collapse. It is still enough for today,
and what will come next will come next.

The same threshing.

ANOTHER PROPITIOUS MOMENT

I know his brown hands
say his plush prayers exactly the same every Friday. He leaves
his phone in a shoe in his room and I hear
the flicker of echo. My voice
as I wait, as it chases itself when he answers. He may think
siren and bell. Or question, void,
ring, noise, interrogation. Every week an aide texts me
a video of Dad in a room with the slightest
outcomes. A bravo. Oh gosh
this is all of him. Then my sister texts me
a new version of guilt. I gallop into my house
on the phone again, my heart rippling
responses, my hands filled with cold
groceries. My father goes waltzing every Thursday
on the tile of the second floor. Eats whatever
they serve him. From 10 to 11 he paints
butterfly hover. What he colors
is superfluous. A drop of pigment. Moments
distracted by the brain's endless hint
or constant hum, he stops falling asleep. He sleeps
in winter or blackberry blossoms. Wakes
to a day or another
with its glances. An aide texts me
a photo of his hands on his cheeks. He looks
west. I know in advance he was not
this charming. His last life exists in still
images. My sister writes
compact sounds. My sister paints
another problem Dad's having, a conclusion, the fog
of his voice. I agree. Last week, Dad explained
three ways to use a zipper:
up, down and the same. Time is an advance
on what we're getting. I pack my red suitcase to get to the opposite

end of the country. Push clothes in each open hole.
From a down escalator, I climb
another whisper. Return to the last
two seconds. On a carpeted floor, I dial again; the phone rings
in his room, in his shoe, unbending its tone.
His breath is steady.
The clock won't hold its ticking.
When he chooses names, the names are some sort of basic
bouquet: daisies and carnations. Easy
to ripple together. He says, *This place is full of doormen.*
This shows me our threshold is an hour:
a slipping. I only think and constantly think
of my father. The future is not what we tell him.

TRAIN OF THOUGHT

Last night in the slow narrative of commuting
noise, I read a woman on a subway car. Her
indelible story, pulled through skin to ink her neck
and arm, vanished at her clavicle. Every word glinted.
I gleaned what I could as the door slid into air,
then closed like a hem. The slouched woman
with her heavy slashes of eyeliner further unrolled
to the plastic curve of the seat. Carbon black letters
turned on her flesh, the half-said singe of bone oil
and naphthol: those disordered thoughts she'd cared
to needle in. The landscape moved around with all
that evidence as the train repeatedly struck tracks,
revising her inscription so everything reflected
through the window became terrain and view,
a readable skin on the land and a shifting
parable of grass and sunset on her shoulder.

THE CHARACTERISTIC FREQUENCY OF FEEDBACK LOOPS

Sweat waltzes the top of his head and I love it!
On the main floor, thirty wheelchairs blunt a sequence of slow escapes
A retired podiatrist is bent left in a black bicycle helmet and keeps circling (fart fart)
All this happens on white linoleum, all the shuffling
Into eternity and the salacious sun
The day is ripped open and soft
Dad scoops his soup with a fork, finds carrots, a crown
How can there be so much to chew and slurp
On this day margarine was patented, made first from beef fat and colored yellow
To seem rich with flavor but I prefer butter
I am in Florida where it is moody July, all reason emptied to a melting point
My father has gained weight and is bigger and does not exist, I mean
Crows trot out from leaves with their ordinary violence and it is impossible
To carry on a conversation in this room
My father opens his hand his mouth
Looks at the light in his hand
I go on, welcoming the last thing or next thing
What if this work is limitless?
This is the best moment, or so we say as the window glass   trembles
With its own echo   and simply   disappears

FATHER TO NARROW THEN STRANGER

I said, *Fix*
your buttons.
He said, *We have to see*

if it is Saturday.
A man with the weight
of belief

in one of his pockets,
and these fill up
fast. He said, *We have to move*

the bodies, and since he was not
broken
by such talk, I endured

his broad
deviance. He said
he would have to—

and when he said it
again, then left it
at that, I smiled

with terrible tangles
in my love. We were told
to expect these

knots. He wanted
it to be
Saturday. He could go vacant

those hidden days

in between. I watched his fingers
scan his glossy picture

on his door. This was all
of him. His fingers formed
his own double

collars, ecstatic
exhausted cheeks. Lost,
you might say,

but we didn't. I said, *The sun*
has again become
rain. I said, *Dad*, and he tried

to arrive
with a new sentence. He said, *Out*
in the earth, time moves

like an angel.
His watch swept

the hours. I said, *Let us*
take what's not
even there. He listened.

SUMMER OF DOWNPOURS AND MOSS

My sister's TV in a fit of light flashes
    the white arms of priests while she sits on the bed
and weeps. Despite her sorry perseverance

at sadness, her mascara still holds and her man stays
    on his knees. I whisper new versions
of the words I've offered before. I do not know

what to say. On the screen, black wings of prayer
    no one notices. The house is choking
hot. I go downstairs. Pour dark coffee into a giant china

chalice. I toast a piece of wheat bread. Butter it
    and deliver it to her lap. It is moist
from the plate. My sister eats in a smear of deep gloom

and begs to know why life's tricks hold
    smaller tricks within. The fan slings
and dangles. She has been crying all this time.

We echo each other: her man and I. We follow
    any line of thought. The day is dark and never
light. And now I have told you a particular story of the heart.

SO MUCH TO REDUCE

We've got three rooms and three days to garbage
or fondle the traces. My husband and I sit
surrounded by letters, maps, locks, coat
pockets, languages. In my father's apartment
we touch each saved paper, his panoramic
past. After eight hours of dust, I stand dizzy
and redolent from all the messages he'd written
in margins—the soft black scrawl of his round
letters and tightening calculations. The rooms
dogged with every vision he had of himself,
with multiple newspapers, unopened
mail, my mother's embroidery (*God don't
make no junk*). In the morning,
we return, probing drawers, making giveaway
piles with unworn dress shirts, shearling coats
with splotches, a vacuum (no hose), stolen
gym towels. I'll never mention any
of this to my father, or I'll lie, or half-lie,
or pretend the apartment is stubbornly
just as he left it. I hold off thinking, just slice open
envelopes. His many mini shampoo bottles
fill me with loneliness. I won't leave this jungle
of items. Down below us, Philadelphia's streetlights
chalk with white, and the bridge grins
brightly across flowing water. My father built
his pleasure and strength from that river
and hummus and meaningless words
and his endless complexities. He always unbent
when he looked from these windows. When dusk claims
the room, we keep on through the abundance:
82 yarmulkes, each curved to his warm
bald head, a monolith of shoes with their wooden
humps, eight-track tapes, three dozen handheld

American flags. I stand at his bedroom door between mercy
and endurance and wish again for this once
boisterous man: his conflict, his rampant
substantial regret. It is almost impossible
to eliminate these acquisitions. The bridge is poised
and the water stealthy, forgotten. His voice lives
here in great detail. He is now lost at the address
I gave him next: beside cupped crocus
jutting up, where the sky shifts from its usual flair
to jumping thunder and the sun holds only one
critical phrase. I gather his bachelor
datebooks fettered in dried rubber bands.
Toupee. 1942 taxes. Cuckoo clocks with their green
eyes. Dark dungarees pressed to a firm line
down the thigh. Broken hats. I turn
my face toward two canisters of sugar. My father—
Yes. No.—When I sleep, I'll hold every
outline, a red sentence, an unusually vivid old word.

UNPREDICTABLE OUTCOME

I can't understand physics. I've been reading a small black book.
Spreading theories of transformation of light.
The curvature of space, the relative universe,
rounder and fuller. Every day is a lump of energy,
the previous day a new block of life.
But when hours lose reason, the equation shuts down.

One cold night, I woke out loud from my alchemical dreams,
not yet ready to let go the persistent vision of tragedy.
It was impossible to imagine any other belief.
I had to wake to salt the wounds. I woke to hold that lack
I had constructed. Went into the hallway where sense
slowly passed into me with its distraction. I sat in the purple lilt.

Before my father was dying but after he had begun
to forget in earnest, I told him, *I love you,* and the velocity of my telling
was something I could cling to. A length, a continuum.
Outside, there was no order, just the earth's old eye
below correlating fields of stars.
The physics book says, *there is no such thing as a real void,*

one that is completely empty. So the earth is in a sort of balance
between people and porch. The start of dawn, the flint
of hummingbirds. Us. Him and me and you.
My dad responded to what I said: *Thank you for the love.*
I keep looking at it. The moment held many particles,
infinitely large and also disappearing.

ORIGINAL HOPE

One borrows time not to be left out.

Been in the pattern of sun—secure, re-creating.
One needs one thing.

One father is left with new limits, but one
father is left. This repeat is filled with above and below.
(Do you understand that it won't cease?)

Every hour compared to dozens of previous
hours and angers, and the daughters post pictures
of vanishing. Such is a comfort.

One agrees to ask for nothing.

Under time lives silence.

FOLK SHOW AT BETTERDAY COFFEE

That Saturday scattered to an urgent sort of ear

as only sodden winter scabbed the floor. At the counter,
the melodic barrage of foam. A timer clicked.

I began to see everything, the brief landscape of booths and the breath
       of a man with an accordion, face full of forehead,
          his hands holding heartbeat, then inhale and exhale. Striped socks,

all the sounds

shrugging up heat —

WHETHER OR NOT OR NEITHER

I call my father every three days on the white
      phone so he can tell me about noon
and its signal. I hold each meander
      up to my head. He has lived past being a particular
being, and I have learned I can love
      longer the last of his vanishing
stories. His steady anxiety splits
      my ghosts, and on Tuesday and Friday
and any day I call him with kindness
      I didn't have years ago. He no longer
settles a sentence. Whatever it's worth, now
      with him I'm all nectar. I've learned to be
sleepless where coyotes find midnight
      desirable. I expect bird forms and forests
to help me recover from the dimming
      of his echoes, that unmanageable
folding. When I was last
      by his sleeve, the woman next to me sobbed
without hesitation every three
      minutes and the orderly
in the chair beside her bent in to her long
      lonely face whispering, *Sandy,*
don't cry. You'll mess up your makeup. Each time
      Sandy was tugged to a quiet and sat perfectly
focused on mist only she
      could see. Outside the window
were here and there some
      gusts. Then, Sandy's plain
lashes fluttered and I saw her eyes
      find the surface and the pattern
of tragedy, which is in me, in you, the drain
      of so much reason,
and the relief of more tears.

AN EYE TO THE OBSTINATE UNENDING

Listen—she said to the light, it's about memory.

Darkest spectacle. The corner
of the bottom. This ecstatic architecture

has opened to an invitation. You believe
you could spend the rest of your life on the porch, finding clues

to the bruising.
You know you couldn't. What is it you want? Aren't you tired
of reflection? If you close one eye, you lose the depth.

When those blues latch, you can focus
on the orbit not in the picture:

worn breeze, quartered windowpanes,
the active gesture of mountains. Any strain, the painted over.

Time now to settle
beyond. See how to see.

IT IS NOT EASY TO LIVE IN MANY

universes. This morning I wanted to see my father
      on my sister's phone screen, wanted
         to show him the street

of my smile, but his mind was full of its almonds.

      The day concentrated its heat. A merciless
rectangular room. When I was a girl, my father could wreck
      an intention, his anger

a gash, and now
                defenseless clear days, when we are
                beautiful

faces. What he supposes we are.
      Scientists use mouse models to understand this disorder.
I am the wise one,

      the fearful one. I read more about mice.
Sometimes I tell my father we're rich
      on bread and orchids. I tell him what is

      a garden, a harbor. Rather than grief, a question
starts at the end. I maze through the latest
      statistics and spend further hours

      with a broom and a teapot. General disintegration.
      Yesterday, in a doctor's office, I saw a photo in *National Geographic*
of rhinos. Through long windows, the ecstatic
      sunshine came into view. I sat in this tired body,

looked at the rhinos. Men had cut off the horns.

I will care
       about everything.
     Those mysterious mammals, those mammoth

gaps in their heads. My father is losing his mind,

      and all the things I know right now
  are what a hole can do. How that hole keeps being empty.

IMPROVISATION ON GEOGRAPHY

When the land passed into our inbox as a series
    of gravities and seedpods and government shapes
to be crossed, no one bothered
    to respond. We owed forty-five percent in taxes
to another country and what we have
    is an absence that has belonged to us
for generations of fathers. Because we never went,
    we must go back through hollowed history
to see even the outline of sun-shudder
    bleaching to visceral light. Let me tell you how
it happened: once
    a man named Mordechai, a man
in my lineage, paid one hundred pounds
    for this plot but feared perhaps
the journey to get there. This is not
    about that man. This is about the future
and the future is that land
    was a hazard to reach. Today I sit with a map
to replenish the past and see how scolding
    the walk, or a trek even done
by cart or goat across fitful sand, oarless
    and gnarled brush. And how else
to arrive with not a dove or king in sight?
    A depth of dust, humanless
wilderness. He was an honest man, a rich man, a man
    making children, a man about
whom I know nothing but mysteries,
    but this I know: he bequeathed that land to Khatoun (wife)
and Rina, Ovadia, Naim—
    each child one-quarter.
I don't think simple pictures. I think
    the downladder and concerto
of that offer. Unwilling, Ovadia and Naim wanted only

their regular Baghdadi streets to repeat days
of skimmed spices, wanted the familiar footpath to the malleable
river. So the land turned to two
remaining—the half
and the half. Yet they too stayed in the pause,
prayers over again. Women continued bending their
knuckles in kitchens, took measure
of flour, neckbones, tiny fig seeds. Each husband thickened
his mustache. Were it not for the children
of these ghosts, also dulling olive, and the children
they'd have, and the slow rise of descendants—
we with our soft feet, broken winters,
strong noses who live on three continents with our perpetual
insomnias—wouldn't know the land now
grows birds where the road folds. Wouldn't know
it is ours regardless of pilgrimage.

ص

IF I TELL YOU HOW DO YOU UNDERSTAND WHY

Someone left a child's red boot in the path.
Done with motion and arrivals, it makes me want
to make a list of trusts.
When I lived in Boston, I dated a bus driver.
We went to a club
where I handed over a fake ID
and the bouncer saw me, young
and soft, a plucked berry. He let me in, knowing
that night I might cloudburst
or underworld. The city was bearable with dirty
habits of snowbanks, tired streets, people at each corner
doubled beside beeches
holding up signs lettered *Hope*. I give
my coats to such suffering. Bus driver bought me a drink
orange with ice. He whispered.
I didn't know what to do
with a man with a mustache. It's ridiculous, the construction
of a memory. The club was dark
and smoky and full of decisions. I can't say
I felt lucky. We left
to walk that old crisp night. Boston was ruined
with slippery weather. He was gentle,
didn't touch me. Dwindling
flakes latched to the ground and I never saw him
again. One hour bent
to another. I had no armor.
I didn't need a map to know where we were going.
And then days went on.
And here I am with the boot, with the desert,
the sun, me beside me in the perfect center
of reason which looks maybe
like nothing, but I call it trust.

CORN AND TURNS

If I won't remember that I was in Virginia last year without praise
of darkness, or the autumn drift I spent in Wisconsin watching a cardinal

nip the oak, if I see and forget field thick over field, the stalks
cut against green—how will I fetch forth the half-dead

memory of the 6 train stuffing its way into the Bronx, as it rolled the same
every day over the florist and the florist's locked gate, over

the circle of urban dirt and suits, and my father emerging
from the chaos at six-eleven pm? My father snugging down the metal,

down to our Buick in a patchwork of misaligned streets. Won't hold
that he always got in on the right with his noise, and now I

never will remember exactly what he said, the layers
of accent crumpled in, and his questions and crusts of amusement that blew

out. Look at all the forgetting I've done, all that I thought I would
always know, though I knew even then the next day

his worn loafers would plod up the stairs to the platform.
I'd hear him go away from us. Again, go above.

ORDER

I call a caterer in another time zone
for platters of whitefish and sliced
tomatoes, fruit salad, forks. *How many?*
the stranger named Eddie says. *Don't know,* I tell him,
curious who will show for my father's
funeral. With my ear to the phone from my home
eight states away, I hear Eddie breathe. He asks, *When
do you need it?* The restaurant behind him hums
and clinks. Those sounds wake me up, make me
glad. What a nice luncheon it will be.
Not sure, I tell Eddie. *It's all
up to my dad.* Perhaps the distant edge
is right next to me. Eddie has an accent. His voice
is soothing with smoke at the ends
of his sentences. *Don't worry anything,* he says.
It's as if he can steady the world I'm suddenly in.
We discuss bread: how much? dark or light? It is casual
business. I hang up and Facetime my dad,
who has been dressed in a bright
orange shirt. He leans against a pillow,
same place he's been for many days. His eyes are open
but the hospice nurse says he can't see. His eyes, brown
for all his life, have turned gray, blue, other silent
colors. Is he permeable? Nothing moves. He is afraid
of death. The mourning doves fumble
outside my window. It is spring. They sing their dubious
defenses. I wish he could still talk to me. Say all
his nothings and donut choices. The stillness
grows loud. I get off the phone and recite the simplest
prayer of future: don't worry anything.
Every day, I see my dad clenching, his hand a fist.
His hand holds everything I am.

PARTIES

On Sunday I wrote the obituary. I paused
before accepting the job, which my brother
gave me because I'm a poet. But it turned out
to be the right thing to do: incident, incident,
life. Windfall, child, marriage. Or none of those.
Instead of focusing on the ghost
in the room, I arranged the data of existence
but left off the intimacies: the figs
and ease, reversals, bothers. Which is to say,
a certainty without the lightning
behavior, his fat thumbs, a nice roundness
to his bald head. How much we would miss.
I couldn't put in reasons or arguments, so I put in
more periods. I slid sentences around
until his life flowed. Decisive, incredibly sound.
I put in what others remembered: dates,
degrees, versions of what you tell people
at parties. I built him a legend:
column-length, tight. Sort of true.

BLADDERPOD, HOUSE LEEK, PRICKLY THRIFT, DRAGONHEAD

I came to the garden to learn a particular name.
Safe harbor the ways water chuckled,
inflating like invisible diamonds.
I came to hear the running
of a small bird. Enough, even
that single gibbering prayer.
Then, the light against pine bark.
I took photos of underneath
because I wanted to see what slipped
between rocks. The mounds and drifts,
the seeds proud to empty. Safe,
next year's dispatch. I could not think more
than silver leaf curl and fritillary cloud,
dappled beginnings. All this landscape
unlike and at the same time exactly
feeling the world. All the plurals and
soft spells growing roots in each other.
When the weather rocked, I listened
to the ordinary and saw it overflow.

LONG AFTER LIGHT

We could not come to an end, no matter how far
we walked, how many rinds of the city we saw,
the sun in wavering ribbons, glassed-in and twisting
off windows. Light to the grease
on the concrete. All day, we were in the world

of enthusiastic pigeons bending to cracks, and the enormous
design, and the fumes, and the architecture, those brown gray
stones. Everywhere, the proximity—tired faces,
incautious and possessive in some way
for the wide intersections, the grace

of the city's deceptions. Complete in networks
of noise, my brother and I, when we had to, turned
against wind lifting graphite from the sidewalks,
to settle to details, to men warm
with waiting to earn the price of a day with successions

of backgammon or swiped handbags. Of course
we've never slept on a sidewalk,
as they have. Of course, I don't know
what my brother has done, but perhaps we've all been
sort of homeless. Somewhere in this insistent arena

someone just failed a fight, another refills
the morphine. City is disappearance—and sleight. More
doorways. And curbs, and let us be clear, every Friday
or Monday, others need to escape the whole hoarse
orbit of languages, complexions,

arbitrary wisdoms. The smell of the scale. The tick
of the sea of such power. And then we were deep down
train tunnels where long slow chords of movement brought us

closer and farther from plenty. How could we leave, but
we did—north to the cemetery

to see the last of our father. To call love
unbearable and cry to the earth, then come back as the plum-
colored sun dipped down, seaming its diligence, handing off
hope to the neon. And we saw the city
muffle such emptiness with its own grand expanse.

ACKNOWLEDGMENTS

My thanks to the editors of the following publications where poems from *Is Is Enough* first appeared, some in slightly different forms:

About Place Journal — "Unpredictable Outcome"

Aperçus — "Long After Light"

At Length — "Elegy for the Routine"

Beloit Poetry Journal — "Father to Narrow then Stranger," "I Pull into the Walgreens Parking Lot," and "It is not easy to live in many"

Blackbird — "Our Daily Ration"

BOAAT — "Probability: Three Cities, Four Minds, Double Entry"

Cave Wall — "If I Tell You How Do You Understand Why"

Construction — "His Kingdom of Brooding"

El Palacio — "Folk Show at Betterday Coffee"

Epiphany — "Goodbye to Aggressions and Generous Gestures"

Gaze – "Another Propitious Moment"

Grist — "Sanctuary"

Harpur Palate — "Summer of Downpours and Moss"

Hobart — "Smeary Flowers, 1983"

J Journal — "Episodic Parallels, More Aunt, Less Moon"

Leavings — "The Characteristic Frequency of Feedback Loops"

Little Patuxent Review — "Train of Thought"

Mid-American Review — "Parties"

On the Seawall — "Strangers in Our Own Earth"

Paperbark — "Given"

Pleiades — "On Harmony"

Poem-A-Day (Academy of American Poets) — "Original Hope"

Post Road — "Fortune"

Psaltery & Lyre — "Bladderpod, House Leek, Prickly Thrift, Dragonhead"

Radar — "Order"

Sugar House Review — "An Eye to the Obstinate Unending"

The Account — "Whether or Not or Neither"

The Common — "Corn and Turns"

The Compass — "So Much to Reduce"

The Los Angeles Review — "Prognosis"

The Maine Review — "The Devotions"

The Rumpus — "Plot Summary"

Women's Studies Quarterly — "Reclaiming Perspective"

"Train of Thought" was translated to Spanish for *Círculo de Poesía*. "On Harmony" was reprinted in *Atelier of Healing: Poetry About Trauma and Recovery* (Squircle Line Press, 2021)."Father to Narrow then Stranger" was reprinted along with a personal essay in *Split This Rock* (2018). The poem was also reprinted in the anthology *In the Tempered Dark: Contemporary Poets Transcending Elegy* (Black Lawrence Press, 2024). "Goodbye to Aggressions and Generous Gestures" was reprinted in *All Night, All Day: Life, Death & Angels* (Madville Publishing, 2023). "Original Hope" was reprinted in *Broken Cord: An Anthology of Writing About Alzheimer's and Dementia* (2021).

NOTES

The Anne Carson epigraph comes from "Thirst: Introduction to Kinds of Water" in *Plainwater* (Vintage, 2000).

The book referenced in "Unpredictable Outcome" is *Seven Brief Lessons on Physics* by Carlo Rovelli (Allen Lane, 2012)

Poems only grow where there is time for them to find their meaning and shape. My thanks to Willowtail Springs, Storyknife Writers Retreat, and Denver Botanic Gardens for awarding me residencies that let me breathe into my phrases and pages.

Gratitude and love to David for holding memory with me, to my siblings for navigating the journey with me, and to you, reader, for listening.

Deepest gratitude to TRP for bringing my father and me into your home.

In memory of Ernest Heskel Mukamal (1935-2019).

ABOUT THE AUTHOR

 **Lauren Camp** is the author of eight previous collections, including *In Old Sky* (Grand Canyon Conservancy, 2024), which grew out of her experience as Astronomer-in-Residence at Grand Canyon National Park. She served as New Mexico Poet Laureate from 2022-25 and founded the New Mexico Epic Poem Project. Honors include fellowships from the Academy of American Poets and Black Earth Institute, a Dorset Prize, a Glenna Luschei Award from *Prairie Schooner*, and finalist citations for the Arab American Book Award and Adrienne Rich Award. Her poems have been translated into Mandarin, Turkish, Spanish, French, and Arabic.

ALSO BY LAUREN CAMP

In Old Sky

Worn Smooth between Devourings

An Eye in Each Square

Took House

Turquoise Door

One Hundred Hungers

The Dailiness

This Business of Wisdom

21ST CENTURY POETS

21st Century Poets is a collection of full-length poetry books by TRP authors whose first book of poetry was released after the year 2000.

BOOKS IN THIS SERIES:

No. 001 – Kendall Dunkelberg – *Time Capsules*

No. 002 – William Bedford Clark – *Blue Norther and Other Poems*

No. 003 – Karla K. Morton – *Names We've Never Known*

No. 004 – Ben Greer – *The Bright House*

No. 005 – Beryl Lawn – *Poems from Both Sides of the Fence*

No. 006 – Swep Lovitt – *Sometimes the World Is Too Beautiful*

No. 007 – William Wright – *Bledsoe*

No. 008 – Sarah Cortez – *Walking Home*

No. 009 – Jesse Graves – *Tennessee Landscape with Blighted Pine*

No. 010 – Richard Boada – *The Error of Nostalgia*

No. 011 – Sarah Cortez – *Cold Blue Steel*

No. 012 – David Havird – *Map Home*

No. 013 – Beryl Lawn – *More Poems from Both Sides of the Fence*

No. 014 – Jesse Graves – *Basin Ghosts*

No. 015 – Karla K. Morton – *A Constant State of Leaping*

No. 016 – Kendall Dunkelberg – *Barrier Island Suite*

No. 017 – Stephen Gibson – *The Garden of Earthly Delights*

No. 018 – Karla K. Morton – *Accidental Origami: New and Selected Works*

No. 019 – Karla K. Morton – *Wooden Lions*

No. 020 – Mary Morris – *Enter Water, Swimmer*

No. 021 – Elisabeth Murawski – *Heiress*